MAKiNG SENSE OF SENSES

Children's Press®
An Imprint of Scholastic Inc.
New York Toronto London Auckland Sydney
Mexico City New Delhi Hong Kong
Danbury, Connecticut

Book production: Educational Reference Publishing

Book design: Nancy Hamlen D'Ambrosio

Science adviser: Jennifer A. Roth, M.A.

Library of Congress Cataloging-in-Publication Data

Making sense of senses.
     p. cm. — (Experiment with science)
  Includes bibliographical references and index.
 ISBN-13: 978-0-531-18540-7 (lib. bdg.)   978-0-531-18760-9 (pbk.)
 ISBN-10: 0-531-18540-0 (lib. bdg.)   0-531-18760-8 (pbk.)
  1. Senses and sensation—Juvenile literature. 2. Senses and
sensation—Experiments—Juvenile literature. I. Title. II. Series.
 QP434.M344 2007
 612.8—dc22
                                    2007015493

1 2 3 4 5 6 7 8 9 10   R   17 16 15 14 13 12 11 10 09 08

CONTENTS

Introduction........................ 4

How Hot Is Hot?
What makes you feel hot or cold? Test the water in this experiment and find out.

6

Can You Hear Me Now?
Hello! Hello! Make two megaphones and have fun with sound waves.

8

Optical Illusions
Fool your eyes—and your brain—with these cool optical illusions.

11

Make a Tongue Map
Where are your taste buds? Stick out your tongue and find out!

14

Afterimages
Find out why you see spots before your eyes when someone takes your picture with a flash camera.

17

Collecting Fingerprints
Become a detective and find out what makes fingerprints unique.

19

Nose Tasting?
You don't use just your sense of taste when you eat. Hold your nose to do this experiment!

22

Are Two Ears Better Than One?
Try this sound experiment and find out the answer.

24

The Science of Scratch 'n' Sniff
In this "spicy" experiment, you'll learn how your sense of smell works.

27

Find Out More..................... 29

Glossary............................. 30

Index................................. 32

MAKiNG SENSE OF SENSES

Our senses provide information about the world around us. Is an ice cube cold? You can sense, or touch, its coldness with your finger. What's that baking in the oven? You can sense, or smell, the aroma even before you sense, or taste, it with your tongue. Is that music coming from the radio? You can sense, or hear, it with your ears, even without sensing, or seeing, the radio with your eyes.

These are the five senses—touch, smell, taste, hearing, and sight. But where do they come from? Humans have special sensory organs. Sensory organs have structures called receptors. These receptors receive messages that are forwarded

Each experiment in this book leads you through the steps you must take to reach a successful conclusion based on scientific results. There are also important symbols you should recognize before you begin your experiment. Here's how the experiments are organized:

Name of experiment

Goal, or purpose, of the experiment

A **You Will Need** box provides a list of supplies you'll need to complete the experiment, as well as the approximate amount of time the experiment should take.

Here's What You Will Do gives step-by-step instructions for working through the experiment.

Here's What's Happening explains the science behind the experiment—and what the conclusion should be.

Mess Factor shows you on a scale of 0 to 5 just how messy the experiment might be (a good thing to know before you begin!).

MESS FACTOR: 3

Science Safety: Whenever you see this caution symbol, read the instructions and be extra careful.

to the brain. The brain decodes the messages in a way that allows you to respond. When you see a ball coming toward you, you know where to go to catch it. You know which way to run when you hear the bell of an ice-cream truck. And when the sweet aroma of fresh-baked cookies meets your nose, you know your way to the kitchen!

In this book, we'll take a look at how the senses are an important part of your everyday life. For example, did you know that your eye has a "blind spot"? Or the reason why you have two ears? Or that things can feel hot and cold at the same time? The experiments in this book will help you to *really* get to know your five senses. You'll learn to map the taste centers on your tongue, collect fingerprints, make a megaphone, and see optical illusions. You'll even make some cool scratch-'n'-sniff cards. So get your eyes, ears, and nose set to go EXPERIMENT WITH SCIENCE!

  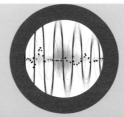  

This symbol means that you should ask an adult to help you or be nearby as you conduct the experiment. Although all the experiments in this book are appropriate and safe for kids to do, whenever you're handling anything that might be sharp or hot, it's important to have adult supervision.

ADULT

In the back of the book, **Find Out More** offers suggestions of other books to read on the subject of senses, and cool Web sites to check out. The **Glossary** (pages 30-31) provides definitions of the highlighted words appearing throughout this book. Finally, the **Index** is the place to go to find exactly what you're looking for.

Here are some important tips before you begin your experiment:

- Check with an adult.
- Read the experiment all the way through.
- Gather everything you need.
- Choose and prepare your "lab" work area.
- Wash and dry your hands.
- Use only clean containers for your experiments.
- Keep careful notes of everything you do and see.
- Stop and ask an adult if you aren't sure what to do.
- When you're finished, clean up your work area completely, and wash your hands!

HOW HOT iS HOT?

YOUR SENSE OF WHAT'S HOT AND WHAT'S COLD DEPENDS ON THE DIFFERENCE IN TEMPERATURE BETWEEN YOUR SKIN AND THE OBJECT YOU TOUCH. FIND OUT WHY IN THIS EXPERIMENT.

Swimming pool water that seems warm to your toes might feel freezing when you jump in.

YOU WiLL NEED

- ❑ 3 bowls
- ❑ water
- ❑ ice cubes

TIME:
10 MINUTES

MESS FACTOR:
2

HERE'S WHAT YOU WILL DO

1 Fill one bowl with ice water, one with hot tap water, and one with room-temperature tap water.

2 Place the fingers of one hand in the ice water, and the fingers of the other hand in the warm water. Wait 30 seconds.

3 Move the hand from the ice water into the room-temperature water. Does it feel warm or cold? Move the hand in the warm water to the room-temperature water. Now how does the water feel?

HERE'S WHAT'S HAPPENING

The heat-sensing nerves in your skin sense differences in temperature. So your fingers that were in the ice water sense room-temperature water as "warm." Your fingers that were in the warm water sense that same water as "cool." The same principle applies to judging the temperature of bathwater. Have you ever put your hand into bathtub water to test the temperature? "Ahh, just right," you think. But then you stick a foot into the water and— "Ouch!" Suddenly it feels too hot. That's because your hands tend to be warmer than your feet when you're standing on a cold bathroom floor.

CAN YOU HEAR ME NOW?

IN THIS EXPERIMENT, YOU WILL AMPLIFY SOUND BY CHANGING HOW SOUND WAVES TRAVEL AND HOW YOUR EARS "CATCH" THEM.

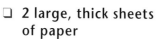

YOU WILL NEED

- ❏ 2 large, thick sheets of paper
- ❏ tape
- ❏ scissors
- ❏ a friend

TIME: 30 MINUTES

MESS FACTOR: 0

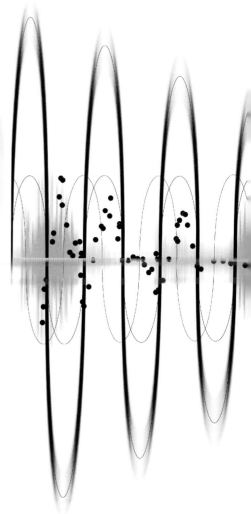

HERE'S WHAT YOU WILL DO

1 Roll one sheet of paper into a cone, with the narrow end an inch or two wide. Tape to hold the shape. Trim the ends so that the cone looks like the megaphone that a cheerleader uses. Repeat with the second piece of paper.

2 Go to an open space with a friend. Have your friend stand in one place with one of the cones within reach. Take the other cone and walk away while your friend talks to you in a loud voice (not quite shouting). Stop at the point where you can no longer hear what he or she is saying.

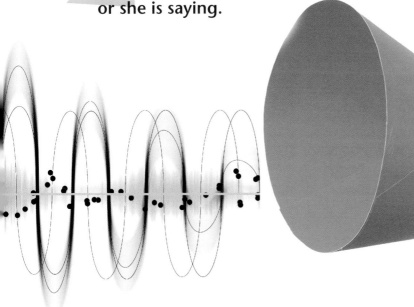

3 Now have your friend speak in the same loud voice—but through the cone, with its wide end pointing straight at you. Can you hear what he or she is saying?

4 As your friend speaks loudly through the cone, move back until you can no longer hear what's being said. Then hold the narrow end of the second cone to one of your ears. Turn so that the wide end of your cone is pointing at your friend's cone. Can you hear the words now?

HERE'S WHAT'S HAPPENING

Sound moves through the air as invisible ripples of energy. These ripples of energy are called sound waves. When sound waves leave their source, they start out close together—like a crowd of runners leaving the starting line. But like runners dashing off in every direction, sound waves spread out rapidly.

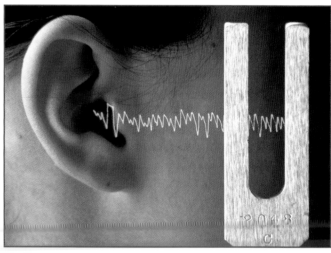

When gently tapped, a tuning fork vibrates producing sound waves (depicted in green) that the brain interprets as a musical note.

In this experiment, your friend's megaphone directed the sound of his or her voice right at you. So instead of spreading out in all directions, more of the sound waves reached your ears. When you put the second cone to your ear, its large end caught more sound waves than your ear could catch by itself. The cone funneled the sound into your ear.

OPTICAL ILLUSIONS

AN OPTICAL ILLUSION IS WHEN YOU THINK YOU SEE SOMETHING THAT'S NOT REALLY THERE. IN THIS EXPERIMENT, YOU'LL PLAY TRICKS ON YOUR BRAIN AND EYES.

BEFORE YOU START

Optical illusions are "mistakes" made by the organs with which you see—your eyes and your brain. Your eyes receive information about the things around you and send this information to the brain. The brain puts it together into something that has meaning for you—even if it differs from what really exists. Let's take a look at some fun optical illusions!

TIME:
10 MINUTES

MESS FACTOR:
0

Read the symbols in the image from left to right.

What symbol do you see in the center? Now scan the symbols in the image from top to bottom. Did the middle symbol change from a letter to a number?

12
ABC
14

Much of what we *think* we see depends on what we *expect* to see. In the row of letters, the brain expects the symbol to be a *B*. In the column of numbers, it expects a *13*.

HERE'S WHAT YOU WILL DO

Hold your pointer fingers a couple of inches apart from each other several inches in front of your eyes, as shown in the picture below. Stare at a distant point beyond your fingers while you slowly bring them closer together. What do you see floating between your fingers?

HERE'S WHAT'S HAPPENING

When you focus into the distance, each of your eyes registers a slightly different image of your two fingers. Your brain interprets the overlapping images from both eyes as a "ghost" finger floating between your real fingers.

 **Look** at the red lines in the two images below. Do they look straight, curved, or at an angle? Are they parallel with each other?

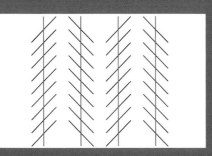 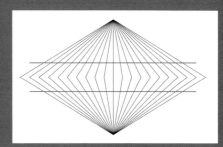

The red lines are all straight and parallel. But the black lines fool the brain into thinking that the red lines are angled or curved.

Hold this page at arm's length. Cover your right eye. With your left eye, stare at the round spot in the image below. Slowly bring the page closer to your face until the square disappears. Now cover your left eye. Stare at the square, and again bring the page slowly closer. Does the round spot disappear?

You've found your blind spot! Every eye has one. It matches a tiny area at the back of each eye that lacks light receptors. The optic nerve enters the eye at this spot.

MAKE A TONGUE MAP

SOUR, SWEET, SALTY, OR BITTER? MAKE A MAP OF THE TASTE CENTERS ON YOUR TONGUE AND DO A TASTE TEST.

YOU WILL NEED

- ❑ 4 small cups
- ❑ teaspoon
- ❑ sugar
- ❑ vinegar
- ❑ baking soda
- ❑ salt
- ❑ cotton swabs
- ❑ glass of water
- ❑ a friend

TIME:
1 HOUR

MESS FACTOR:
1

A
Bitter

B
Sour

C
Salty

D
Sweet

HERE'S WHAT YOU WILL DO

1 Make a chart like the one shown below. Notice that each letter matches a certain area on the tongue map on page 14 (A for bitter, B for sour, C for salty, and D for sweet).

2 In each cup, place a teaspoon of one of the following: sugar (for sweet), vinegar (sour), baking soda (bitter), and salt (salty).

3 Moisten a cotton swab in water. Roll the tip in one of the substances, but don't tell your friend which one it is. Ask your friend to stick out his or her tongue. Touch the swab lightly to each of the four areas shown on the tongue map. Be sure to get something on each spot.

4 On your chart, place a plus sign (+) in the box that matches the tongue area where your friend senses the taste most strongly.

tongue map

	A	B	C	D
sugar				
vinegar				
baking soda				
salt				

WHAT'S UMAMI?

Many scientists believe there is a fifth basic taste called *umami*. Umami means "delicious" in Japanese. The taste is often described as "meaty."

5 Using fresh cotton swabs, repeat steps 3 and 4 for each of the other test substances. Then switch with your friend to get your results.

Do you think that different parts of the tongue are more sensitive to certain tastes? Did your results differ from those on the tongue map?

HERE'S WHAT'S HAPPENING

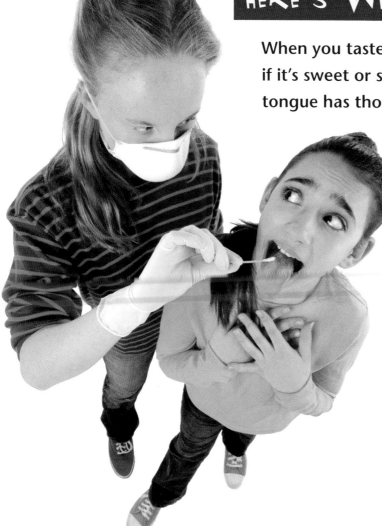

When you taste something, you instantly know if it's sweet or sour, right? That's because your tongue has thousands of tiny bumps, called 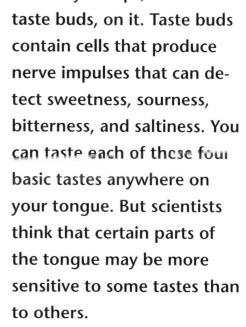 taste buds, on it. Taste buds contain cells that produce nerve impulses that can detect sweetness, sourness, bitterness, and saltiness. You can taste each of these four basic tastes anywhere on your tongue. But scientists think that certain parts of the tongue may be more sensitive to some tastes than to others.

AFTERIMAGES

AFTERIMAGES ARE OPTICAL ILLUSIONS THAT SHOW HOW OUR EYES DETECT LIGHT AND COLOR. DO THIS EXPERIMENT TO FIND OUT ABOUT TWO KINDS OF AFTERIMAGES.

YOU WILL NEED

- ❏ 3"x 5" index card
- ❏ scissors
- ❏ markers in bold colors
- ❏ pencil
- ❏ tape

TIME: 10 MINUTES

MESS FACTOR: 3

HERE'S WHAT YOU WILL DO

1 Capture the Bird
Cut the index card in half. In the middle of one piece, draw a simple bird. In the middle of the other piece, draw a cage that fits your bird.

2 Tape the cards together, back-to-back. Leave a gap in the middle to insert the pencil. Securely tape the cards near one end of the inserted pencil.

3 Quickly rub the pencil between your palms to spin the pictures back and forth in front of you. Have you captured the bird in the cage?

HERE'S WHAT'S HAPPENING

Have you ever seen a big spot float before your eyes after someone took your picture with a flash camera? That spot is an example of an optical illusion called an afterimage. You see images when light enters your eyes and produces chemical changes in the retina. These changes stay for a moment to produce afterimages that you seldom notice. But in this experiment, when you twirl the pencil fast enough, the afterimages of the bird and cage overlap. You "see" them as one image.

CATCH THE FISH

Stare at the white and orange fish for 20 seconds. (Count slowly!) Then shift your gaze to the fishbowl and blink once or twice. Did a light-colored fish appear in the bowl?

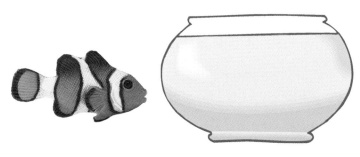

We see colors because of chemical changes in cone cells in the eye's retina. When you stare at colors for a long time, you temporarily reduce the cone chemicals that detect those colors. So when you look away, you see a negative afterimage that lacks these colors. That's why the white and orange fish looks like a light-colored fish in the bowl!

COLLECTING FINGERPRINTS

BE A DETECTIVE AND MAKE YOUR OWN FINGERPRINTS. THEN SEARCH FOR HIDDEN FINGERPRINTS IN YOUR CLASSROOM OR HOME.

YOU WILL NEED

- ❏ ink pad
- ❏ white index cards
- ❏ cornstarch
- ❏ cocoa powder
- ❏ soft paintbrush
- ❏ magnifying glass (optional)

TIME: 30 MINUTES

MESS FACTOR: 4

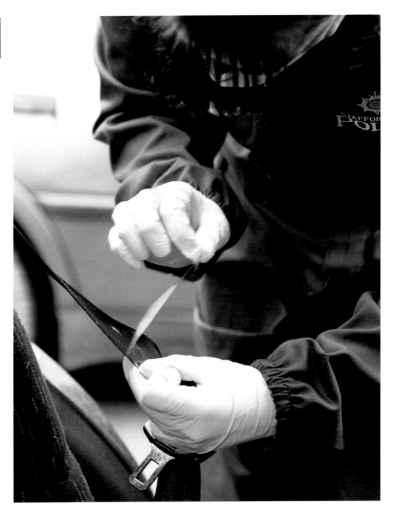

This police officer is using tape to lift a fingerprint from a car seat belt. Criminals often leave their fingerprints at the scene of a crime.

HERE'S WHAT YOU WILL DO

1 Gently but firmly press and roll the tip of your pointer finger on the ink pad. You want ink on the top half inch of your finger.

2 Press one edge of your finger on an index card, and roll your finger, once, from one side to the other (not back and forth!).

3 Can you see your fingerprint? If it's too smeared, repeat steps 1 and 2 until you get a clear print.

loop

4 Look for patterns in your fingerprint. A magnifying glass helps. Do you see examples of the loops, whorls, or arches shown in the illustrations at left?

whorl

5 Compare your prints to those of friends and family. Whose do your fingerprints look like—the prints of your friends or those of your family members?

arch

HERE'S WHAT'S HAPPENING

Can you think of activities that don't involve your sense of touch? There aren't many. Fingerprints are an important way to identify people. And they're used as evidence by detectives to help solve crimes. In this experiment, the ridges on your fingers picked up the ink and transferred it to the white card, making a visible print. Children's fingers and prints get bigger as they age, but the patterns don't change. No two people have the same fingerprint. But basic patterns such as whorls and loops tend to run in families.

INVESTIGATION VARIATION:

1 Look for small objects in your classroom or home that have smudges left after someone touched them. Some good examples are drinking glasses, jars, and shiny folders.

2 Over a sink or newspaper, sprinkle a small amount of "fingerprint powder" onto the smudges. Use the cornstarch on dark objects, and the cocoa powder on light or clear objects. Gently brush off excess powder with your paintbrush. Can you see a fingerprint? Smooth surfaces are usually better at capturing fingerprints than surfaces that are rough or bumpy.

NOSE TASTING?

FIND OUT HOW YOUR SENSE OF SMELL INFLUENCES YOUR SENSE OF TASTE.

Your sense of smell affects your sense of taste. A lemon won't taste so sour if you hold your nose!

YOU WILL NEED

- ❑ food grater
- ❑ apple
- ❑ potato
- ❑ carrot
- ❑ cucumber
- ❑ large plate
- ❑ blindfold
- ❑ 2 forks
- ❑ a friend

TIME: 30 MINUTES

HERE'S WHAT YOU WILL DO

Grate the four foods into separate piles on the plate. Put on the blindfold. Gently but firmly pinch your nose closed.

MESS FACTOR: 1

2 Ask your friend to feed you a forkful of each food. See if you can identify them. Switch and, with a fresh fork, see if your friend can tell the foods apart.

HERE'S WHAT'S HAPPENING

Have you ever wondered why nothing tastes great when you have a cold? Or why it helps to hold your nose when you have to eat something yucky? The taste buds of the tongue can tell whether something is sweet, sour, salty, or bitter. But our sense of smell adds important detail to what we think of as flavor. Normally, a food's smell reaches your nose at the same time that you taste the food on your tongue. So, if you hold your nose, you'll have trouble identifying a food's flavor.

ARE TWO EARS BETTER THAN ONE?

IT IS EASIER TO TELL WHERE A SOUND IS COMING FROM WITH TWO EARS. THIS EXPERIMENT WILL HELP YOU UNDERSTAND WHY.

With two ears, we can not only recognize sound, but we can also locate it and estimate its distance.

Safety First!
Never push anything into your ear, and never make loud noises into a tube pointing near someone's ear.

YOU WILL NEED

- ❑ scarf or other blindfold
- ❑ 3 or more friends
- ❑ pen or pencil
- ❑ 3-foot flexible tube or hose

 TIME: 15 MINUTES

MESS FACTOR: 0

HERE'S WHAT YOU WILL DO

1 Sit or stand in the center of a circle of friends. Tie a scarf or other blindfold around your eyes or keep them tightly closed. (No peeking!)

2 With one hand, cover one ear. Have your friends take turns clapping, one at a time, while you use your other hand to point in the direction of the clapper. Are your friends laughing? Open your eyes. Are you pointing in the wrong direction?

3 Do the same experiment with both ears uncovered. Is it easier to locate the person clapping? Is it still hard to locate clapping coming from certain positions in the circle?

A TUBULAR VARIATION

1 Hold the ends of a 3-foot (.9-meter) flexible tube close to your ears, as shown on the next page. Close your eyes.

2 Ask a friend to *gently* tap on the outside of the tube in different places. Can you tell when your friend is tapping in the middle of the tube? To the left side? To the right?

3 Drop the tubing from one ear and try the test again using just one ear. Is it harder to tell where on the tube your friend is tapping?

HERE'S WHAT'S HAPPENING

When you hear with both ears, your brain uses two important sensory clues to locate the sound. One clue is that the sound reaches one ear a fraction of a second before it reaches the other ear. The other clue is that the sound is slightly louder in the ear that faces the sound source. So even with both ears, it can be hard for a blindfolded person to locate a sound that's the same distance from both ears. That includes noises coming from someone directly in front of or behind your head.

When you hold the tube to both ears, it should be easy to tell where your friend is tapping. But when you try the test with only one ear, it's hard to figure out where the sound is coming from.

THE SCIENCE OF SCRATCH 'N' SNIFF

THIS EXPERIMENT WILL SHOW YOU HOW "SCRATCH-'N'-SNIFF" STICKERS RELEASE THEIR ODOR WHEN YOU SCRATCH THEM.

YOU WILL NEED

- ❏ pen or pencil
- ❏ index cards
- ❏ glue (nontoxic and unscented)
- ❏ powdered spices such as:
  - cinnamon
  - nutmeg
  - garlic
  - curry

TIME: 1 DAY

MESS FACTOR: 1

HERE'S WHAT YOU WILL DO

Write the name of each spice on the back of an index card. Spread a thin layer of nontoxic glue on the front of each card. While the glue's still wet, sprinkle it with the spice you listed on the back of the card. Gently shake the cards over a trash can to get rid of the spice that doesn't stick. Let the cards dry overnight.

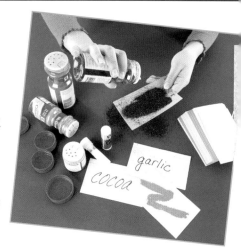

Without looking at the back of each card, hold it several inches from your nose and sniff. Can you identify the spice? Don't peek at the answer yet!

Now scratch the spice on the dried glue and sniff again. Is the smell stronger and easier to identify?

HERE'S WHAT'S HAPPENING

Your sense of smell depends on invisible chemicals traveling from the source of the odor through the air and entering your nose. Inside your nose, these chemicals come in contact with cells that send a "smell" signal to your brain. When you rubbed the spiced glue on your cards, you released some of the spice chemicals into the air. This made the odor strong. The makers of scratch-'n'-sniff stickers capture scents on paper in much the same way. When you scratch the sticker, you release the chemicals.

FiND OUT MORE

To find more information on the science of senses, check out these books and Web sites:

BOOKS

Auch, Alison J. *That's Hot!* Compass Point Books, 2002.

Gold, Martha V. *The Nervous System.* Enslow, 2004.

Hewitt, Sally. *It's Science: The Five Senses.* Scholastic, 1999.

Jones, Charlotte Foltz. *Fingerprints and Talking Bones: How Real-Life Crimes Are Solved.* Bantam Doubleday Dell, 1999.

Murphy, Patricia J.; Nanci R. Vargus; and Beth Cox. *Sight.* Scholastic, 2003.

Parker, Steve. *Our Bodies: The Senses.* Raintree, 2004.

Pringle, Laurence. *Hearing; Smell; Taste.* Marshall Cavendish/Benchmark, 1999.

Sherman, Josepha. *Ear: Learning How We Hear.* Rosen, 2002.

Viegas, Jennifer. *Eye: Learning How We See; Mouth and Nose: Learning How We Taste and Smell.* Rosen, 2002.

WEB SITES

Seeing, Hearing, and Smelling the World
www.hhmi.org/senses/
Seeing, hearing, smelling, touching, and tasting require billions of specialized cells. Learn the fascinating ways your brain and your sense organs "talk" to each other at this site presented by the Howard Hughes Medical Institute.

The Exploratorium's Online Exhibits
www.exploratorium.edu/exhibits/f_exhibits.html
Find several online exhibits of fascinating optical illusions. From the Exploratorium.

The Franklin Institute—Minutes from ME—Tasting
sln.fi.edu/qa97/me12/me12.html
Learn how you taste flavors, and find out what parts of your tongue are sensitive to foods that are bitter, sour, sweet, and salty.

WonderNet—Smell and Taste
www.chemistry.org/portal/a/c/s/1/wonder netdisplay.html?DOC=wondernet%5Cwhat sup%5Csmell%5Cwu_smell.html
Try some activities to learn fascinating facts about how your sense of smell works. Also, discover why food doesn't seem very tasty when your nose is stuffed up from a cold. From the American Chemical Society.

WonderNet—Sound and Hearing
www.chemistry.org/portal/a/c/s/1/wondernet display.html?DOC=wondernet%5Cactivities %5Csound%5Csound.html
Did you know that the making of a sound and the way we hear sounds have to do with vibrations? Try some activities to learn more about this amazing phenomenon. From the American Chemical Society.

GLOSSARY

A

afterimages images that persist after the original source is no longer active.

amplify to increase the loudness of sound.

arches curves that rise in the middle.

B

blind spot the point on the retina, not sensitive to light, where the optic nerve leaves the eyeball.

C

cells basic, microscopic parts of an animal or a plant.

chemicals substances produced by or used in chemistry.

cone cells cells in the retina that produce color vision.

E

energy power, or the ability to make something change or move. Forms of energy include light, heat, and electricity.

F

fingerprints the unique patterns left by the ridges on a finger.

flavor the overall sensation of food, combining taste and aroma.

i

impulses short, sudden bursts or flows.

L

loops curves with ends that meet.

M

megaphone a cone-shaped device used to amplify and direct the voice.

N

nerves cells that convey messages to the brain.

nontoxic not poisonous; safe to use.

O

odor a sensation detected by the nose; also called aroma or scent.

optical illusions images we see that are deceptive or misleading.

optic nerve the nerve that connects the retina of the eye to the brain.

P

parallel lying in the same plane and the same distance apart at all points.

principle a basic truth, law, or belief.

R

receptors cells or nerves that detect a particular chemical or force.

registers indicates or shows automatically.

retina the light-sensitive tissue lining the back of the eye.

S

sensitive able to feel and respond to slight changes.

sensory relating to the organs in the body that receive information from its surroundings. The human sense organs include the eyes, ears, nose, taste buds, and skin.

sound waves traveling vibrations perceived as sound when they strike the ear.

spice flavorful plant powders used in food.

swab a small piece of cotton attached to the end of a stick.

T

taste buds clusters of cells in the tongue that sense whether something is sweet, sour, salty, or bitter.

temperature a measure of heat energy.

W

whorls patterns of complete circles.

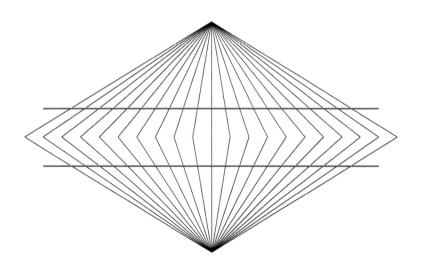

Pictures are shown in **bold**.

afterimages 17-**18**

blind spot 13

brain 10, 11, 12, 13, 26, 28

cells, cone 18

color 17, 18

ears 8, **10**, **24**, 25-26

energy 10

eyes 11, **12**, 13, 17, 18

fingerprints **19**, 20, **21**
    arch **20**
    loop **20**, 21
    whirl **20**, 21

flavor 23

hands 7

hearing, sense of 8-10,
   24-26

heat 7

ice **7**

impulse, nerve 16

ink 20-21

light 17, 18

magnifying glass **21**

megaphone **8**, **9**, 10

nose 22, 23, 28

optical illusions **11-13**, 17

optic nerve 13

receptor 13

retina 18

scientist 16

scratch 'n' sniff **27**-28

senses
    hearing 8-10, 24-26
    sight 11-13, 17-18
    smell 22-23, 27-28
    taste 14-16, 22-23
    touch 6-7, 19-21

sight, sense of 11-13

skin 6, 7

smell, sense of 22-23,
   27-28

sound 8, 10, 24, 26

sound waves 8, 10

spice 28

taste, sense of 14-16, 22-23

taste buds 16, 23

temperature 6, 7

tongue **14**, 15-16, 23

touch, sense of 6-7, 19-21

tuning fork **10**

umami 15

voice 9, 10

water **6**, 7

Photographs © 2008: Alamy Images/Images Etc. Ltd.: 5 right center, 6; Getty Images: page headers (Alex Bloch), 5 left, 15 top (Jan Greune), 22 (Scott Hancock); Photo Researchers, NY: 10 (Oscar Burriel), 19 (Michael Donne), 4 left center, 24 (Phil Jude), 3 center left, 5 center, 8 right, 9 left (Mehau Kulyk), 4 right, 20 bottom left, 20 bottom left, 20 bottom left (Alfred Pasieka), 1, 13 top right, 13 top left, 31 bottom (Science Photo Library); Richard Hutchings Photography: back cover, cover, 3 top center right, 3 bottom right, 3 bottom left, 3 top, 4 right center, 5 left center, 5 right, 7, 8 left, 9 right, 12, 14, 16, 17, 18, 20 right, 20 top, 21, 23, 25, 26, 28 bottom, 28 top.